Influential Environment and Resources Cases in China

(Volume I)

中国具有影响力环境资源案件

（第一辑）

中华人民共和国最高人民法院环境资源审判庭 编著

Environment and Resources Division of the Supreme People's Court of the People's Republic of China

人民法院出版社

长城（图片来源：Pixabay）
The Great Wall（Photo: Pixabay）

中国具有影响力环境资源案件

（第一辑）

Influential Environment and Resources Cases in China

(Volume I)

编者按
Editor's Note

编者按

生态文明是人类社会进步的重大成果，是实现人与自然和谐共生的必然要求。中国政府高度重视生态文明建设，把生态文明建设作为关系中华民族永续发展的根本大计，坚持绿水青山就是金山银山的理念，开展了一系列根本性、开创性、长远性的工作，美丽中国建设迈出重要步伐，推动我国生态环境保护发生历史性、转折性、全局性变化。

环境司法是环境治理体系的重要一环，在推进环境治理和生态文明制度建设中发挥着不可替代的重要作用。中国最高人民法院于2014年6月设立环境资源审判庭，负责审理重大环境资源案件，指导全国法院环境资源审判工作，推动构建专业化的环境资源审判体系。截至2022年10月，全国各级法院共设立环境资源审判庭、合议庭和人民法庭2400余个。中国法院通过完善审判体制机制，加强审判队伍建设，健全审判程序规则，依法公正高效审理各类环境资源案件203余万件，为推进生态文明建设和绿色发展提供坚强有力的司法服务和保障。

呵护美丽地球、建设美好家园是人类共同愿望。中国法院积极开展中外环境司法合作，尤其注重加强在环境司法案例领域的交流。最高人民法院和联合国环境规划署于2017年9月签订谅解备忘录，商定在联合国环境规划署法律数据库建立专门的中国环境司法裁判板块，由最高人民法院选送环境资源案例和环境司法白皮书在网站上发布，将优秀的中国环境司法裁判文书与世界各国共享。首批收录的10个案例及2016年、2017年发布的《中国环境资源审判》白皮书英文版已于2019年3月入库。

本书系将首批发布于联合国环境规划署法律数据库的 10 个环境资源案例集结成册。这 10 个案例是从最高人民法院历年发布的环境资源典型案例中选取，包括刑事、民事、行政、公益诉讼各种类型，涵盖大气、水、土壤、矿产、林业、渔业、野生动物等环境要素，对于统一中国环境资源案件裁判标准，完善审理规则，发挥司法的评价指引和政策形成功能起到了重要作用。相信案例英文版的出版对于传播中国环境司法声音，加强中外环境司法案例交流和研究，必将起到积极的推动作用。这里，要感谢欧洲环保协会的支持，使得本书得以顺利面世。

文明因交流而多彩，文明因互鉴而丰富。当前，中国正处于全面深化生态文明体制改革、全面建设社会主义现代化国家的新征程中，中国各级法院在习近平生态文明思想指引下奋力前行。在这个过程中，我们既要立足本国国情、坚持自身特色，又要吸收借鉴世界各国司法文明成果。中国最高人民法院希望通过在国际环境司法领域充分交流、务实合作，为维护全球生态安全、构建人类命运共同体作出积极贡献。

最高人民法院环境资源审判庭

2022 年 11 月

Editor's Note

Ecological civilization is a great accomplishment of human society and the inevitable pathway to harmonious coexistence between human and nature. Therefore, China attaches great importance to the development of an ecological civilization, making it a fundamental plan for the sustainable development of the nation. Under the guiding principle of "green is gold," we have undertaken fundamental, ground-breaking, and long-term endeavors that have brought us closer to a beautiful China with historical, transitional, and all-encompassing changes in ecological environmental protection. The Chinese government attaches great importance to the construction of ecological civilization and has made it a fundamental plan for the sustainable development of the Chinese nation.

Environmental justice, integral to the environmental governance system, plays an irreplaceable role in building ecological civilization system. In June 2014, the Supreme People's Court of China set up a specialized Environment and Resources Division to hear major environment and resources cases and guide the environmental adjudication across the court system. Since then, specialized environmental divisions and tribunals have been created within courts of all levels. By the end of year 2022, a total of over 2,400 environment and resources divisions, collegial panels and tribunals had been established across China. The court system, with sound adjudication rules, a well-designed mechanism and ever more experienced judges, have provided sound judicial safeguards for ecological civilization and green development.

It is the shared aspiration of mankind to protect the mother earth and build a beautiful home. China's court system has been active in collaborating with its international counterparts in environmental adjudication, with focus on stepping up the sharing and studying of environmental cases. In September 2017, the Supreme People's Court and the UN Environment Programme signed the Memorandum of Understanding to create a Chinese environmental adjudication section in the UN Environment Programme's global online law database, where example cases and white papers on environmental justice will be selected by the Supreme People's Court and then published on the database and shared across the world. The English translation of the first batch of 10 example cases and the White Paper of "China's Environment and Resources Adjudication" 2016, 2017 were already released on the online database on

March, 2019.

This book is a collection of the 10 environment and resources cases published in the UN Environment Programme's environmental law database. These 10 cases are selected amongst the environment and resources guiding cases issued by the Supreme People's Court over the previous years, including criminal, civil, administrative, public interest litigations and actions for ecological damages and involving environmental elements such as air, water, soil, minerals, forestry, fisheries, wildlife and so on. Sharing guiding cases as such can help set a uniform standard and improved rules for environmental adjudication, and strengthen the role of law in behavior guiding and policy formulation. The English publication is believed to be another active step towards publicity of China's environmental justice and more in-depth international exchanges and study on environmental cases. I would like to take this opportunity to thank ClientEarth China, for the publication would not happen without their support.

Civilizations thrive as they learn from each other. China is at a critical stage of comprehensively deepening the reform of ecological civilization system and has embarked on a new journey to fully build a modern socialist country. Courts of all levels are making strides under the guidance of Xi Jinping's thought of ecological civilization. At this juncture, we must absorb and learn from the judicial civilizations of other countries while bearing in mind our national conditions and sticking to Chinese characteristics. The Supreme People's Court hopes to contribute to global ecological security and the building of a community with a shared future for mankind through in-depth exchanges and fruitful cooperation in the field of international environmental justice.

Environment and Resources Division
Supreme People's Court
People's Republic of China
November 2022

目录
Table of Contents

云南梯田（图片来源：Pixabay）

Rice Terraces, Yunnan Province(Photo: Pixabay)

一、南京某染料有限公司、王某荣等污染环境案

【基本案情】

南京某染料有限公司（以下简称某染料公司）生产过程中产生的废酸液体属于危险废物，依照国家相关规定应当交由具有资质的企业进行处置。2010 年 9 月，王某受某染料公司指派联系处置废酸事宜，与仅具有经销危险化学品资质的南京某化工有限公司（以下简称某化工公司）法定代表人王某荣达成了以每吨 580 元处置废酸的口头协议。此后，某染料公司产生的废酸液体均交由王某荣进行处置。时任公司罐区主管的黄某军明知某化工公司王某荣没有处置资质，仍具体负责与拉运废酸的王某荣直接对接，王某负责审核支付处置废酸费用。2013 年 9 月，王某荣明知丁某东（另案处理）没有处置废酸资质，仍与丁某东达成每吨 150 元处置费用的口头协议，并指使被告人徐某米驾驶槽罐车从某染料公司拉运废酸，直接送至丁某东停放在江都宜陵码头等处的船上。至 2014 年 5 月间，交由丁某东处置的废酸共计 2828.02 吨。期间，丁某东多次指使被告人孙某山、钱某林等人于夜间驾驶船只，将其中的 2698.1 吨废酸直接排放至泰东河和新通扬运河水域的河道中。其中，孙某山参与排放 1729.82 吨，钱某林参与排放 318.78 吨。后丁某东未及时排放的

某染料公司罐区现场照片（图片来源：审理法院）

长江江苏段（图片来源：审理法院）

129.92 吨废酸被查获。江苏科技咨询中心、江苏省环境科学研究院专家论证分析认为，某染料公司产生的上述废酸液体属于危险废物，其中主要成份为硫酸并含有大量有机物，硫酸浓度较高且具有极强的腐蚀性，对生物、水体、环境的危害极大，废酸中残存的大量有机废物对生物环境也会造成长远的累积性危害。

【裁判结果】

江苏省高邮市人民法院一审认为：被告单位某染料公司违反国家环境保护法律规定，明知被告人王某荣经营的某化工公司无废酸处置资质，将公司生产过程中产生的废酸交由王某荣处置；被告人王某荣明知丁某东亦无废酸处置资质，仍将某染料公司的废酸转交其处置；被告人徐某米明知其运输的是化工废液以及丁某东可能没有处置废酸的能力，而帮助王某荣进行运输作业；被告人孙某山、钱某林明知是化工废液，仍然违反国家规定偷排，最终导致严重污染环境的后果，均已构成污染环境罪，且属共同犯罪。被告人王某、黄某军是某染料公司直接负责的主管人员和其他直接责任人员，应当知道王某荣没有废酸处置资质，仍然在各自职责范围内促成交易，导致严重污染环境的后果发生，均应以污染环境罪追究刑事责任。某染料公司为降低危险废物的处置成本，在明知他人没有处置资质的情况下仍委托进行处置，最终导致严重污染环境，某染料公司由此减少支出巨额的处置费用。一审法院综合某染料公司的犯罪情节以及缴纳罚金的能力，以污染环境罪判处某染料公司罚金 2000 万元，判处其余被告人一年至五年有期徒刑不等并处罚金。江苏省扬州市中级人民法院二审维持原判。

【典型意义】

本案是因非法处置危险废物污染水体引发的环境污染刑事案件，对于根据罪责刑相适应原则妥当确定单位犯污染环境罪的罚金数额进行了有益探索。根据《中华人民共和国刑法》规定，判处罚金，应当根据犯罪情节决定罚金数额。对于单位罚金的确定，应当根据单位犯罪的情节和特点，结合单位违法所得数额、造成损失的大小等因素综合考虑。某染料公司为降低危险废物的处置成本，明知他人没有处置资质仍委托进行处置，最终导致严重污染环境后果的发生，由此逃避支付的巨额处置费用可认定为通过犯罪行为获取的利益。同时，消除环境污染的严重后果必然会有相当多的费用支出，根据相关司法解释规定，公私财产损失包括污染环境行为直接造成财产损毁、减少的实际价值，以及为防止污染扩大、消除污染而采取必要合理措施所产生的费用，故而，公私财产损失数额应当作为确定罚金的一个重要参数。人民法院根据某染料公司的犯罪情节以及缴纳罚金的能力，在实际获取利益和公私财产损失数额的区间幅度内确定判处罚金的数额，既有利于生态环境的修复，也有助于充分发挥刑罚威慑力，督促企业提高依法处置危险废物的自觉性。

【审理法院及合议庭成员】

一审：江苏省高邮市人民法院 吴家明、嵇晓红、陈兆辉

二审：江苏省扬州市中级人民法院 尹晓涛、李春蓉、郝佳佳

二、何某强等非法杀害珍贵濒危野生动物、非法狩猎刑事附带民事诉讼案

【基本案情】

2014 年 11 月至 2015 年 1 月期间，何某强、钟某军在湖南省东洞庭湖国家级自然保护区收鱼时，与养鱼户及帮工人员方某华、龙某如、龙某明和涂某保、余某秋、张某海、任某平等人商定投毒杀害保护区内野生候鸟，由何某强提供农药并负责收购。此后，何某强等人先后多次在保护区内投毒杀害野生候鸟，均由何某强统一收购后贩卖给李某介绍的汪某平。2015 年 1 月 18 日，何某强、钟某军先后从方某华及余某秋处收购了 8 袋共计 63 只候鸟，在岳阳市君山区壕坝码头被自然保护区管理局工作人员当场查获。经鉴定，上述 63 只候鸟均为中毒死亡，其中 12 只小天鹅及 5 只白琵鹭均属国家二级保护野生动物，其余苍鹭、赤麻鸭、赤颈鸭、斑嘴鸭、夜鹭等共计 46 只，均属国家“三有”保护野生动物。查获的 63 只野生候鸟核定价值为 44 617 元。

湖南省岳阳市岳阳楼区人民检察院以何某强等七人犯非法猎捕、杀害珍贵濒危野生动物罪，向岳阳市岳阳楼区人民法院提起公诉。岳阳市林业局提起刑事附带民事诉讼，请求七名被告人共同赔偿损失 53 553 元，湖南省岳阳市岳阳楼区人民检察院支持起诉。

【裁判结果】

湖南省岳阳市岳阳楼区人民法院一审认为，何某强伙同钟某军、方某华在湖南东洞庭湖国家级自然保护区内，采取投毒方式非法杀害国家二级保护动物小天鹅、白琵鹭及其它野生动物，李某帮助何某强购毒并全程负责对毒杀的野生候鸟进行销售，何某强、钟某军、方某华、李某的行为均已构成非法杀害珍贵、濒危野生动物罪，属情节特别严重。龙某如、龙某明、龙某在何某强的授意下，采取投毒方式，分别在国家级自然保护区内猎杀野生候鸟，破坏野生动物资源，情节严重，其行为均已构成非法狩猎罪。何某强、钟某军的犯罪行为同时触犯非法杀害珍贵、濒危野生动物罪和非法狩猎罪，应择一重罪以非法杀害珍贵、濒危野生动物罪定罪处罚。此外，因何某强等七人的犯罪行为破坏了国家野生动物资源，致使国家财产遭受损失，

各方应承担赔偿责任。相应损失涉案 63 只野生候鸟的核定价值认定为 44 617 元，根据各人在犯罪过程中所起的具体作用进行分担。遂判决何某强、钟某军、方某华、李某犯非法杀害珍贵、濒危野生动物罪，判处有期徒刑六年至十二年不等，并处罚金；龙某如、龙某、龙某明犯非法狩猎罪，判处有期徒刑一年至二年不等，其中二人缓刑二年；由何某强等七人共同向岳阳市林业局赔偿损失 44 617 元。宣判后，部分被告人提出上诉，湖南省岳阳市中级人民法院驳回上诉，维持原判。

【典型意义】

本案为非法猎捕、杀害珍贵、濒危野生动物刑事附带民事诉讼案件。刑罚是环境治理的重要方式，面对日趋严峻的环境资源问题，运用刑罚手段惩治和防范环境资源犯罪，加大环境资源刑事司法保护力度，是维护生态环境的重要环节。本案发生于东洞庭湖国家级自然保护区内，在检察机关提起公诉的同时，由相关环境资源主管部门提起刑事附带民事诉讼，检察机关支持起诉，依法同时追究行为人刑事责任和民事责任，具有较高借鉴价值。一审法院在认定七名被告人均具有在自然保护区内投毒杀害野生候鸟的主观犯意前提下，正确区分各自的客观行为，根据主客观相一致原则对七名被告人分别以杀害珍贵、濒危野生动物罪和非法狩猎罪定罪，并根

小天鹅（摄影：周洋）

麋鹿群奔跑在东洞庭湖国家级自然保护区（图片来源：《湖南日报》）

据共同犯罪理论区分主从犯，分别对七名被告人判处一年至十二年不等的有期徒刑，部分适用缓刑，既体现了从严惩治环境资源犯罪的基本价值取向，突出了环境法益的独立地位，又体现了宽严相济的刑事政策，充分发挥了刑法的威慑和教育功能。此外，本案不仅追究了被告人杀害野生候鸟的刑事责任，还追究了被告人因其犯罪行为给国家野生动物资源造成损失的民事赔偿责任，对环境资源刑事犯罪和民事赔偿案件的一并处理具有较好的示范意义。

【审理法院及合议庭成员】

一审：湖南省岳阳市岳阳楼区人民法院 肖冰峰、李林、文建设

二审：湖南省岳阳市中级人民法院 任燕、喻蓓蓓等

白琵鹭（图片来源：Saifuddin Ratlamwala/Pexels）

三、江苏省某环保联合会诉泰兴某化工有限公司等水污染民事公益诉讼案

【基本案情】

2012 年 1 月至 2013 年 2 月，被告泰兴某化工有限公司（以下简称某化工公司）等六家企业将生产过程中产生的危险废物废盐酸、废硫酸总计 2.5 万余吨，以每吨 20 元至 100 元不等的价格，交给无危险废物处理资质的相关公司偷排进泰兴市如泰运河、泰州市高港区古马干河中，导致水体严重污染。江苏省某环保联合会（以下简称某环保联合会）诉请法院判令某化工公司等六家被告企业赔偿环境修复费 1.6 亿余元、鉴定评估费用 10 万元。

【裁判结果】

江苏省泰州市中级人民法院一审认为，某环保联合会作为依法成立的参与环境保护事业的非营利性社团组织，有权提起环境公益诉讼。六家被告企业将副产酸交给无处置资质和处置能力的公司，支付的款项远低于依法处理副产酸所需费用，导致大量副产酸未经处理倾倒入河，造成严重环境污染，应当赔偿损失并恢复生态环境。2 万多吨副产酸倾倒入河必然造成严重环境污染，由于河水流动，即使倾倒地点的水质好转，并不意味着河流的生态环境已完全恢复，依然需要修复。在修复费用难以计算的情况下，应当以虚拟治理成本法计算生态环境修复费用。遂判决六家被告企业赔偿环境修复费用共计 1.6 亿余元，并承担鉴定评估费用 10 万元及诉讼费用。

江苏省高级人民法院二审认为，某环保联合会依法具备提起环境公益诉讼的原告资格，一审审判程序合法。六家被告企业处置副产酸的行为与造成古马干河、如泰运河环境污染损害结果之间存在因果关系。一审判决对赔偿数额的认定正确，修复费用计算方法适当，六家被告企业依法应当就其造成的环境污染损害承担侵权责任。二审判决维持一审法院关于六家被告企业赔偿环境修复费用共计 1.6 亿余元的判项，并对义务的履行方式进行了调整。如六家被告企业能够通过技术改造对副产酸进行循环利用，明显降低环境风险，且一年内没有因环境违法行为受到处罚，其已支付的技术改造费用可经验收后在判令赔偿环境修复费用的 40% 额度内抵扣。六

家被告企业中的三家在二审判决后积极履行了判决的全部内容。某化工公司不服二审判决，向最高人民法院申请再审。

最高人民法院认为，环境污染案件中，危险化学品和化工产品生产企业对其主营产品及副产品均需具有较高的注意义务，需要全面了解其主营产品和主营产品生产过程中产生的副产品是否具有高度危险性，是否会造成环境污染；需要使其主营产品的生产、出售、运输、储存和处置符合相关法律规定；亦需使其副产品的生产、出售、运输、储存和处置符合相关法律规定，避免对生态环境造成损害或者产生造成生态环境损害的重大风险。虽然河水具有流动性和自净能力，但在环境容量有限的前提下，向水体大量倾倒副产酸，必然对河流的水质、水体动植物、河床、河岸以及河流下游的生态环境造成严重破坏。如不及时修复，污染的累积必然会超出环境承载能力，最终造成不可逆转的环境损害。因此，不能以部分水域的水质得到恢复为由，免除污染者应当承担的环境修复责任。最高人民法院最终裁定驳回了某化工公司的再审申请。

【典型意义】

泰州水污染公益诉讼案被媒体称为“天价”环境公益诉讼案。该案由社会组织作为原告、检察机关支持起诉，参与主体特殊、涉案被告多、判赔金额大、探索创新

如泰运河（图片来源：如皋市人民政府网站）

多、借鉴价值高。一审法院正确认定某环保联合会的主体资格，确认某化工公司等六家公司主观上具有非法处置危险废物的故意，客观上造成了环境严重污染的结果，应该承担对环境污染进行修复的赔偿责任。同时，结合鉴定意见和专家意见认定环境修复费用，判令六家被告企业共计赔偿 1.6 亿余元环境修复费用。二审法院衡平企业良性发展与环境保护目标，创新了修复费用支付方式，鼓励企业加大技术改造力度，处理好全局利益与局部利益、长远利益与短期利益的关系，承担起企业环境保护主体责任和社会责任。最高人民法院肯定了二审法院创新修复费用支付方式的做法，鼓励企业积极开展技术创新和改造，促进区域生态环境质量改善。同时明确了危险化学品和化工产品生产企业在生产经营过程中应具有较高的注意义务，应承担更多的社会责任。对于河水这种具有流动性和自净能力的环境介质，确立了水污染环境修复责任的处理原则，即污染行为一旦发生，不因水环境的自净改善而影响污染者承担修复义务。本案对水污染案件的处理具有示范意义。

【审理法院及合议庭成员】

一审：江苏省泰兴市中级人民法院 纪阿林、叶志军、蔡鹏、王健祥、王亚光

二审：江苏省高级人民法院 刘建功、陈迎等

再审审查：最高人民法院 林文学、魏文超、刘小飞、吴凯敏等

泰州市（图片来源：视觉中国）

庭审现场（图片来源：审理法院）

四、中国某环保基金会诉宁夏某科技股份有限公司等腾格里沙漠污染系列民事公益诉讼案

【基本案情】

2015 年 8 月，中国某环保基金会（以下简称某环保基金会）向一审法院提起诉讼称，宁夏某科技股份有限公司等八家企业在生产过程中违规将超标废水直接排入蒸发池，造成腾格里沙漠严重污染，截至起诉时仍然没有整改完毕。请求判令：（1）停止非法污染环境行为；（2）对造成环境污染的危险予以消除；（3）恢复生态环境或者成立沙漠环境修复专项基金并委托具有资质的第三方进行修复；（4）针对第 2 项和第 3 项诉讼请求，由法院组织原告、技术专家、法律专家、人大代表、政协委员共同验收；（5）赔偿环境修复前生态功能损失；（6）在全国性媒体上公开赔礼道歉。某环保基金会向法院提交了基金会法人登记证书，显示其是在国家民政部登记的基金会法人。某环保基金会提交的 2010 年至 2014 年年度检查证明材料显示其在提起本案公益诉讼前五年年检合格。某环保基金会提交了五年内未因从事业务活动违反法律、法规的规定而受到行政、刑事处罚的无违法记录声明。此外，某环保基金会章程规定，其宗旨为“广泛动员全社会关心和支持生物多样性保护和绿色发展事业，保护国家战略资源，促进生态文明建设和人与自然和谐，构建人类美好家园”。某环保基金会还向法院提交了其自 1985 年成立至今，一直实际从事包括举办环境保护研讨会、组织生态考察、开展环境保护宣传教育、提起环境民事公益诉讼等活动的相关证据材料。

【裁判结果】

宁夏回族自治区中卫市中级人民法院一审认为，某环保基金会不能认定为《中华人民共和国环境保护法》第五十八条规定的“专门从事环境保护公益活动”的社会组织，对某环保基金会的起诉裁定不予受理。某环保基金会不服，提起上诉。宁夏回族自治区高级人民法院审查后裁定驳回上诉，维持原裁定。某环保基金会不服二审裁定，向最高人民法院申请再审。

最高人民法院依法提审并审理认为，因环境公共利益具有普惠性和共享性，没有特定的、法律上的直接利害关系人，有

腾格里沙漠与黄河（图片来源：robertharding / Alamy Stock Photo）

必要鼓励、引导和规范社会组织依法提起环境公益诉讼，以充分发挥环境公益诉讼功能。依据《中华人民共和国环境保护法》第五十八条和《最高人民法院关于审理环境民事公益诉讼案件适用法律若干问题的解释》第四条的规定，对于本案某环保基金会是否可以作为“专门从事环境保护公益活动”的社会组织提起本案诉讼，应重点从其宗旨和业务范围是否包含维护环境公共利益，是否实际从事环境保护公益活动，以及所维护的环境公共利益是否与其宗旨和业务范围具有关联性三个方面进行审查。对于社会组织宗旨和业务范围是否包含维护环境公共利益，应根据其内涵而非简单依据文字表述作出判断。社会组织章程即使未写明维护环境公共利益，但若其工作内容属于保护各种影响人类生存和发展的天然的和经过人工改造的自然因素的范畴，均应认定宗旨和业务范围包含维护环境公共利益。某环保基金会章程中规定的宗旨契合绿色发展理念，亦与环境保护密切相关，属于维护环境公共利益的范畴。环境保护公益活动，不仅包括植树造林、濒危物种保护、节能减排、环境修复等直接改善生态环境的行为，还包括与环境保护有关的宣传教育、研究培训、学术

腾格里沙漠绿洲（图片来源：视觉中国）

交流、法律援助、公益诉讼等有利于完善环境治理体系，提高环境治理能力，促进全社会形成环境保护广泛共识的活动。某环保基金会在本案一审、二审及再审期间提交的历史沿革、公益活动照片、环境公益诉讼立案受理通知书等相关证据材料，虽未经庭审质证，但在立案审查阶段，足以显示环保基金会自 1985 年成立以来长期实际从事包括举办环境保护研讨会、组织生态考察、开展环境保护宣传教育、提起环境民事公益诉讼等环境保护活动，符合前述法律和司法解释的规定。同时，上述证据亦证明该组织从事环境保护公益活动的时间已满五年，符合《中华人民共和国环境保护法》第五十八条关于社会组织从事环境保护公益活动应五年以上的规定。依据《最高人民法院关于审理环境民事公益诉讼案件适用法律若干问题的解释》第四条的规定，社会组织提起的公益诉讼涉及的环境公共利益，应与社会组织的宗旨和业务范围具有一定关联。即使社会组织起诉事项与其宗旨和业务范围不具有对应关系，但若与其所保护的环境要素或者生态系统具有一定的联系，亦应基于关联性标准确认其主体资格。本案环境公益诉讼是针对腾格里沙漠污染提起。沙漠生物群落及其环境相互作用所形成的复杂而脆弱的沙漠生态系统，需要人类的珍惜利用和悉心呵护。某环保基金会起诉认为宁夏某科技股份有限公司将超标废水排入蒸发池，严重破坏了腾格里沙漠本已脆弱的生态系统，所涉及的环境公共利益维护属于某环保基金会宗旨和业务范围。此外，某环保基金会提交的基金会法人登记证书、年度检查证明材料、无违法记录声明等，证明其符合《中华人民共和国环境保护法》第五十八条及《最高人民法院关于审理环境民事公益诉讼案件适用法律若干问题的解释》第二条、第三条、第五条对提起环境公益诉讼社会组织的其他要求，具备提起环境民事公益诉讼的主体资格。最高人民法院再审裁定撤销一审、二审裁定，指令本案由中卫市中级人民法院立案受理。

【典型意义】

最高人民法院通过审理腾格里沙漠污染系列民事公益诉讼案，针对《中华人民共和国环境保护法》修订以来各地环境公益诉讼案件审理中出现的与原告主体资格有关的突出问题，就《中华人民共和国环境保护法》第五十八条以及《最高人民法院关于审理环境民事公益诉讼案件适用法律若干问题的解释》规定的环境公益诉讼原告主体资格相关法律适用问题，确立、细化了裁判规则。再审裁定明确，对于社会组织是否具备提起环境民事公益诉讼的主体资格，应当重点从宗旨和业务范围是否包含维护环境公共利益，是否实际从事环境保护公益活动，以及所维护的环境公共利益是否与其宗旨和业务范围具有关联性三个方面进行认定。再审裁定阐明对于社会组织宗旨和业务范围是否包含维护环境公共利益，应根据其内涵而非简单依据文字表述作出判断；阐明了环境保护公益活动，不仅包括直接改善生态环境的行为，还包括有利于完善环境治理体系，提高环境治理能力，促进全社会形成环境保护广泛共识的活动；阐明了社会组织起诉事项与其宗旨和业务范围即便不具有对应关系，但若与其所保护的环境要素或者生态系统具有一定的联系，亦应基于关联性标准确认其主体资格。该系列案件是最高人民法院首次通过具体案例从司法层面就环境民事公益诉讼主体问题明确判断标准，推动了环境公益诉讼制度的发展，已作为最高人民法院指导性案例发布，对于环境民事公益诉讼案件的审理具有重要的指引和示范作用。

【审理法院及合议庭成员】

再审审查：最高人民法院 刘小飞、叶阳、吴凯敏

五、北京市朝阳区某环境研究所、福建省某环境某中心诉谢某锦等四人破坏林地民事公益诉讼案

【基本案情】

2008 年 7 月 29 日，谢某锦等四人未经行政主管部门审批，擅自扩大采矿范围，采取从山顶往下剥山皮、将采矿产生的弃石往山下倾倒、在矿山塘口下方兴建工棚的方式，严重毁坏了 28.33 亩林地植被。2014 年 7 月 28 日，谢某锦等人因犯非法占用农用地罪分别被判处刑罚。2015 年 1 月 1 日，北京市朝阳区某环境研究所、福建省某环境某中心提起诉讼，请求判令四被告承担在一定期限内恢复林地植被的责任，赔偿生态环境服务功能损失 134 万元；如不能在一定期限内恢复林地植被，则应赔偿生态环境修复费用 110 万余元；共同偿付原告为诉讼支出的评估费、律师费及其他合理费用。

【裁判结果】

福建省南平市中级人民法院一审认为，谢某锦等四人为采矿占用林地，不仅严重破坏了 28.33 亩林地的原有植被，还造成了林地植被受损至恢复原状期间生态服务功能的损害，依法应共同承担恢复林地植被、赔偿生态功能损害的侵权责任。遂判令谢某锦等四人在判决生效之日起五个月内恢复被破坏的 28.33 亩林地功能，在该林地上补种林木并抚育管护三年，如不能在指定期限内恢复林地植被，则共同赔偿生态环境修复费用 110 万余元；共同赔偿生态环境服务功能损失 127 万元，用于原地或异地生态修复；共同支付原告支出的评估费、律师费、为诉讼支出的其他合理费用 16.5 万余元。福建省高级人民法院二审维持了一审判决。

【典型意义】

本案为《中华人民共和国环境保护法》于 2014 年修订后全国首例环境民事公益诉讼，涉及原告主体资格的审查、环境修复责任的承担以及生态环境服务功能损失的赔偿等问题。本案判决依照《中华人民共和国环境保护法》第五十八条和《最高人民法院关于审理环境民事公益诉讼案件适用法律若干问题的解释》的规定，确认了社会组织作为公益诉讼原告的主体资格；以生态环境修复为着眼点，判令被告限期恢复被破坏林地功能，在该林地上补种林

木并抚育管护三年，进而实现尽快恢复林地植被、修复生态环境的目的；首次通过判决明确支持生态环境受到损害至恢复原状期间服务功能损失的赔偿请求，提高了破坏生态行为的违法成本，体现了保护生态环境的价值理念，判决具有很好的评价、指引和示范作用。

【审理法院及合议庭成员】

一审：福建省南平市中级人民法院 林东波、甘代兴、张廷贵、黄慧勤、朱峰

二审：福建省高级人民法院 祝昌霖、李和平、林锦斌

福建省光泽县华桥乡何舟坪村（摄影：王楠）

福建省光泽县华桥乡何舟坪村（摄影：王楠）

六、江苏省徐州市人民检察院诉徐州市某造纸有限公司水污染民事公益诉讼案

【基本案情】

徐州市某造纸有限公司（以下简称某造纸公司）多次被环境保护主管机关查获以私设暗管方式向连通京杭运河的苏北堤河排放生产废水，废水的化学需氧量、氨氮、总磷等污染物指标均超标。江苏省徐州市铜山区环境保护局曾两次对某造纸公司予以行政处罚。徐州市人民检察院作为公益诉讼人，于 2015 年 12 月 28 日提起环境民事公益诉讼，请求判令某造纸公司将被污染损害的苏北堤河环境恢复原状，并赔偿生态环境受到损害至恢复原状期间的服务功能损失；如某造纸公司无法恢复原状，请求判令其以 2600 吨废水的生态环境修复费用 26.91 万元为基准，以该基准的 3 倍至 5 倍承担赔偿责任。

【裁判结果】

江苏省徐州市中级人民法院一审认为，某造纸公司排放废水污染环境，应当承担环境污染责任。根据已查明的环境污染事实、某造纸公司的主观过错程度、防治污染设备的运行成本、生态环境恢复的难易程度、生态环境的服务功能等因素，可酌情确定该公司应当承担的生态环境修复费用及生态环境受到损害至恢复原状期间的服务功能损失，遂判决某造纸公司赔偿生态环境修复费用及服务功能损失共计 105.82 万元。宣判后，某造纸公司以一审公益诉讼人徐州市人民检察院为被上诉人提起上诉。江苏省高级人民法院二审认为，污染物排放点的环境质量已经达标不能作为某造纸公司拒绝承担生态环境修复费用的理由，一审判决以 2.035 倍作为以虚拟治理成本法计算生态环境修复费用的系数并无不当，以查明的某造纸公司排放废水量的 4 倍计算生态环境修复费用具有事实和法律依据。二审判决驳回上诉，维持原判。

【典型意义】

本案是全国人大常委会授权检察机关试点提起公益诉讼以来人民法院依法受理的首批民事公益诉讼案件之一，也是人民法院审理的第一起检察机关试点提起公益诉讼的二审案件。一审法院注重司法公开，体现公众参与，合议庭由审判员和人民陪审员共同组成，庭审向社会公开并进行视

暗管排放污染废水进入河流（图片来源：Dmitriy Prayzel/Shutterstock）

频、文字同步直播。庭审时邀请专家辅助人就环境保护专业技术问题提出专家意见，较好地解决了环境资源案件科学性和公正性的衔接问题。本案尝试根据被告违法排污的主观过错程度、排污行为的隐蔽性以及环境损害后果等因素，合理确定生态环境修复费用，加大污染企业违法成本，有助于从源头上遏制企业违法排污。二审法院依据《中华人民共和国民事诉讼法》及《全国人民代表大会常务委员会关于授权最高人民检察院在部分地区开展公益诉讼试点工作的决定》审理检察机关提起公益诉讼的二审案件，对于完善该类案件二审程序规则起到了示范作用。

【审理法院及合议庭成员】

一审：江苏省徐州市中级人民法院 蔡可勇、李娟、陈虎、徐树启、周晓云

二审：江苏省高级人民法院 陈迎、臧静、赵黎

江苏白马湖（图片来源：淮安市白马湖旅游区网站）

七、某环保联合会诉德州某有限公司大气污染民事公益诉讼案

【基本案情】

德州某有限公司（以下简称某公司）是一家从事玻璃及玻璃深加工产品制造的企业，位于山东省德州市。某公司虽投入资金建设脱硫除尘设施，但仍有两个烟囱长期超标排放污染物，造成大气污染，严重影响了周围居民生活，被环境保护部点名批评，并被山东省环境保护行政主管部门多次处罚，但其仍持续超标向大气排放污染物。某环保联合会提起诉讼，请求：判令某公司立即停止超标向大气排放污染物，增设大气污染防治设施，经环境保护行政主管部门验收合格并投入使用后方可进行生产经营活动；赔偿因超标排放污染物造成的损失 2040 万元（诉讼期间变更为 2746 万元）及因拒不改正超标排放污染物行为造成的损失 780 万元，并将赔偿款项支付至地方政府财政专户，用于德州市大气污染的治理；在省级及以上媒体向社会公开赔礼道歉；承担本案诉讼、检验、鉴定、专家证人、律师及其他为诉讼支出的费用。山东省德州市中级人民法院受理本案后，向某公司送达民事起诉状等

空气污染
（图片来源：Predrag Mladenovic/Shutterstock）

城市清洁空气（图片来源：Mckyartstudi–Shutterstock）

诉讼材料，向社会公告案件受理情况，并向德州市环境保护局告知本案受理情况。德州市人民政府、德州市环境保护局积极支持、配合本案审理，并与一审法院共同召开协调会。通过司法机关与环境保护行政主管部门的联动、协调，某公司将全部生产线关停，在远离居民生活区的天衢工业园区选址建设新厂，防止了污染及损害的进一步扩大，使案件尚未审结即取得阶段性成效。

【裁判结果】

山东省德州市中级人民法院一审认为，诉讼期间某公司放水停产，停止使用原厂区，可以认定某公司已经停止侵害。在停止排放前，某公司未安装或者未运行脱硫和脱硝治理设施，未安装除尘设施或者除尘设施处理能力不够，多次超标向大气排放二氧化硫、氮氧化物、烟粉尘等污染物。其中，二氧化硫、氮氧化物是酸雨的前导物，过量排放形成酸雨会造成居民人身及财产损害，过量排放烟粉尘将影响大气能见度及清洁度。某公司超标排放污染物的行为导致了大气环境的生态附加值功能受到损害，应当依法承担生态环境修复责任，赔偿生态环境受到损害至恢复原状期间服务功能损失。同时，某公司超标向大气排放污染物的行为侵害了社会公众的精神性环境权益，应当承担赔礼道歉的民事责任。遂判决某公司赔偿超标排放污染物造成损失2198.36万元，用于大气环境质量修复；某公司在省级以上媒体向社会公开赔礼道歉等。宣判后，双方当事人均未提起上诉，一审判决已生效。

【典型意义】

德州大气污染公益诉讼案是《中华人民共和国环境保护法》修订后，人民法院受理的首例京津冀及其周边地区大气污染公益诉讼案件。大气具有流动性，其本身具有一定的自净功能，企业超标排放是否构成生态环境损害是本案审理的难点。本案裁判明确超标过量排放二氧化硫、氮氧化物和粉尘将影响大气的生态服务功能，应当承担法律责任，可根据企业超标排放数量以及二氧化硫、氮氧化物和粉尘的单位治理成本计算大气污染治理的虚拟成本，进而作为生态环境损害赔偿的依据，具有一定合理性。某公司在本案审理期间主动承担社会责任，积极采取措施防止污染的持续和扩大，值得肯定。本案的审结及时回应了当前社会公众对京津冀及周边地区的大气污染治理的关切，对区域大气污染治理进行了有益的实践探索。

【审理法院及合议庭成员】

一审：山东省德州市中级人民法院 刘立兵、张小雪、高晓敏

八、四川某矿业有限公司诉新疆某资源投资股份有限公司特殊区域合作勘查合同纠纷案

【基本案情】

2011 年 10 月 10 日，新疆某资源投资股份有限公司（以下简称某投资公司）与四川某矿业有限公司（以下简称某矿业公司）签订《合作勘查开发协议》，约定：某投资公司补偿某矿业公司 3500 万元后，双方共同设立项目公司，并在符合条件时

塔什库尔干（图片来源：塔什库尔干县政府办公室）

塔什库尔干（图片来源：塔什库尔干县政府办公室）

将某矿业公司探矿权过户至项目公司名下。2011 年 10 月 25 日，某投资公司向某矿业公司实际支付 3500 万元。2013 年 11 月 22 日，某投资公司以合作勘查作业区位于新疆塔什库尔干野生动物自然保护区为由通知解除合同，某矿业公司回函拒绝。某矿业公司提起诉讼，请求确认某投资公司解除合同行为无效并确认《合作勘查开发协议》有效。某投资公司反诉请求解除《合作勘查开发协议》，某矿业公司返还合作补偿款 3500 万元并赔偿损失。

【裁判结果】

新疆维吾尔自治区高级人民法院一审判决某投资公司解除合同行为无效，双方继续履行《合作勘查开发协议》，驳回某投资公司的反诉请求。最高人民法院二审认为，案涉探矿权位于新疆塔什库尔干野生动物自然保护区范围内，该自然保护区设立在先，某矿业公司的探矿权取得在后，基于《合作勘查开发协议》约定，双方当事人均知道或者应当知道在自然保护区内不允许进行矿产资源的勘探和开发。该协议违反了《中华人民共和国自然保护区条例》的禁止性规定，如果认定协议有效并继续履行，将对自然环境和生态造成严重破坏，损害环境公共利益。故协议依法应属无效，某矿业公司收取的 3500 万元合作补偿款应予返还。某投资公司主张的损失，部分由某矿业公司折价补偿，部分由某投资公司自行承担或者在项目公司清算时另行解决。二审法院撤销一审判决，予以改判。

【典型意义】

在自然保护区、风景名胜区、重点生态功能区、生态环境敏感区和脆弱区等特殊区域内，环境保护与经济发展之间的矛盾较为突出。人民法院审理、执行相关案件，要依据国家和省级国土空间主体功能

区规划，充分考虑各类功能区的不同功能定位，确定不同的处理思路。对于优化开发区域尤其是重点开发区域发生的环境资源纠纷，可以更多地考虑合理利用环境容量发展经济的需要，对于限制开发和禁止开发区域，尤其是在划定生态保护红线地区发生的环境资源纠纷，则要贯彻最严格的保护措施。针对上述特殊区域签订的勘查、开采矿产资源合同，即使已经得到国土资源主管部门批准，人民法院仍应对合同效力进行特别审查，若合同违反法律、行政法规的强制性规定，损害环境公共利益的，应依法认定无效。本案确立的裁判规则对于自然资源开发利用合同的效力审查具有示范意义。

【审理法院及合议庭成员】

二审：最高人民法院 王季君、晏景、朱婧

九、贵州某生态养殖开发有限公司诉贵州某铝业有限公司财产损害赔偿案

【基本案情】

贵州某生态养殖开发有限公司（以下简称某养殖公司）是一家主要从事鲟鱼养殖的企业，从戈家寨大沟取水。贵州某铝业有限公司（以下简称某铝业公司）于2014年10月在戈家寨水库上游河段筑坝取水。由于某铝业公司筑坝拦水，下游河道水量减少，导致某养殖公司养殖的鲟鱼在4月21日至23日因严重缺水缺氧大量窒息死亡。某养殖公司主张，某铝业公司从事工程建设，明知对原有供水水源有不利影响，应当采取相应的补救措施。某铝业公司在未通知下游用水户做好应对准备的情况下，擅自蓄水断水，造成某养殖公司养殖的鲟鱼缺氧窒息大量死亡。某养殖公司诉至法院，主张某铝业公司承担赔偿责任。

【裁判结果】

贵州省清镇市人民法院一审认为，河流生态流量可以保证河流所需的自净扩散能力，维持水生生态系统平衡，保证库区养殖业所需的水质水量。我国虽然没有关于河流生态流量的法律规定，但实践中有此要求，如水电站最小下泄流量就是保障河流生态流量的措施。某铝业公司未办理取水行政许可及进行环境影响评价，擅自修建拦截坝取水，未保障必要的生态下泄流量，导致下游水量减少，养殖场进水减少，鲟鱼窒息死亡。故某养殖公司养殖的鲟鱼死亡与某铝业公司蓄水之间存在因果关系，判决某铝业公司赔偿某养殖公司经济损失757 158.6元。某铝业公司不服，提起上诉。贵阳市中级人民法院二审判决驳回上诉、维持原判。

鲟鱼（图片来源：DIGITALSHAPE/shutterstock）

某铝业公司下泄生态流量，下游河道水流正常（图片来源：审理法院）

养殖公司正常取水养鱼（图片来源：审理法院）

【典型意义】

长江流域蕴藏着十分丰富的水资源，依法审理水资源开发利用案件，促进水资源可持续利用是人民法院环境资源审判的重要职责。本案是水资源开发利用过程中产生的侵权纠纷，涉及到水资源利用中“生态流量”的保障和控制。河流生态流量具有重要价值，上游地区用水户在水资源开发和利用过程中，要保障河流生态流量，不能损害下游地区供水、通航、灌溉、养殖等生态流量受益方的合法权益，从而保障全流域水生生态系统基本功能的正常运转。本案中，作为主要从事鲟鱼养殖的某养殖公司与某铝业公司均为戈家寨水库的需水方，均应依照法律规定取水、用水、排水。某铝业公司在上游取水、用水时未办理取水行政许可和进行环境影响评价，擅自修建拦截坝取水，未保障必要的生态下泄流量，损害了下游用水户的合法权益，导致损害事实的发生，依法应当承担赔偿责任。本案肯定了生态流量的重要价值，维护了生态流量受益方的合法权益，对于人民法院审理水资源开发利用案件具有指导意义。

【审理法院及合议庭成员】

一审：贵州省清镇市人民法院 罗光黔、李云鹤、张奇

二审：贵州省贵阳市中级人民法院 曾桢、唐玉平、马劼

十、海南某水务有限公司诉海南省某生态环境保护局环保行政处罚案

【基本案情】

2013 年 6 月 5 日，海南省环境监测中心站出具琼环监字 [2013] 第 153 号《监测报告》（以下简称 153 号《监测报告》）。海南省某生态环境保护局（以下简称某环保局）根据 153 号《监测报告》，认为海南某水务有限公司（以下简称某水务公司）涉嫌违法排放水污染物，于 2014 年 4 月 16 日拟对某水务公司作出行政处罚。某水务公司在法定期限内未提出陈述、申辩和听证的申请。同年 6 月 16 日，某环保局作出被诉儋土环资罚决字 [2014]47 号《行政处罚决定书》(以下简称 47 号处罚决定)，对某水务公司处以 2013 年 5 月应缴纳排污费二倍的罚款 177 719 元。某市人民政府经复议后对 47 号处罚决定予以维持。某水务公司不服，遂诉至法院，请求撤销 47 号处罚决定。

【裁判结果】

海南省儋州市人民法院一审认为，某环保局作为当地环境保护工作的行政主管部门，具有对本辖区内违法排放水污染物的行为作出行政处罚的法定职权。根据《环境行政处罚办法》第三十四条的规定，采样是本案监测的必经程序。但某环保局未能提供采样记录或采样过程等相关证据，无法证明其采样程序合法，进而无法证明送检样品的真实性，直接影响监测结果的真实性。因此，某环保局在没有收集确凿证据证实样品来源真实可靠的情况下，仅以海南省环境监测中心站出具的 153 号《监测报告》认定某水务公司超标排放废水，主要证据不足。某环保局于 2014 年 6 月 16 日同时分别对某水务公司 2013 年 1 月 14 日和 5 月 22 日超标排放行为给予二次处罚，程序违法。被诉 47 号处罚决定只给予某水务公司罚款，未责令某水务公司限期改正，行政处罚行为明显不当。一审法院判决撤销 47 号处罚决定，由某环保局承担诉讼费用。海南省第二中级人民法院二审认为，153 号《监测报告》的合法性是审查本案被诉环保行政处罚事实认定是否清楚的基础。由于 153 号《监测报告》的取样程序违法，不能作为认定某水务公司存在环境违法行为事实的主要证据。而除 153 号《监测报告》外，某环保局没有进

海南省儋州市（图片来源：苏晓杰 / 海南日报）

行相关调查，并且违反查处分离的规定，程序违法。47号处罚决定认定事实的主要证据不足，适用法律错误。二审法院判决驳回上诉，维持原判。

【典型意义】

本案为环保行政处罚纠纷，涉及对环保行政处罚行为所依据证据的审查认定，具有典型性和指导意义。近年来，各级环保行政执法部门加大对生态环境违法案件的行政执法力度，有效遏制了环境恶化态势。但从法院审理环境行政处罚案件情况看，环保行政执法中存在执法不规范，“重结果、轻程序”等问题。环保行政执法部门在环境监测过程中，应重视环境监测程序的合法性，特别是在涉及水污染的环保处罚案件中，被检测标本的取样是否合乎技术规范，直接影响该标本检测结果正确与否。因此，《环境行政处罚办法》专门对现场调查取样程序作出规定，要求制作取样记录或者将取样过程记入现场检查（勘察）笔录，并可以采取拍照、录像或者其他方式记录取样情况。本案中，由于某环保局在一审中未能提供取样记录或取样过程等相关证据，无法证明其取样程序的合法性，故法院认定153号《监测报告》不能作为认定某水务公司存在环境违法行为事实的主要证据，依法撤销处罚决定。本案判决体现了人民法院对环保行政执法行为的监督，对于推动环境保护行政主管部门规范行使行政处罚职权、促进依法行政具有积极作用。

【审理法院及合议庭成员】

一审：海南省儋州市人民法院 王清华、王波、刘耀雄

二审：海南省第二中级人民法院 张德雄、文魁兴、刘霞

I. Environmental Pollution Case against Nanjing ** Dyeing Company, Wang *rong et al

[Basic Facts]

The waste acid liquid generated in the production process of Nanjing ** Dyeing Company (hereinafter referred to as"the dyeing company")is a type of hazardous waste and should be delivered to qualified enterprises for disposal according to relevant provisions of the state. In September 2010, the dyeing company appointed Wang * to coordinate the disposal of the waste acid –Wang * then reached a verbal agreement with Wang *rong, the legal representative of Nanjing ** chemicals company (hereinafter referred to as "the chemicals company"), on disposal of the waste acid at the price of CNY 580 per ton. However, the company was only qualified for distribution of hazardous chemicals, rather than disposal. Thereafter, the waste acid liquid generated by the dyeing company was delivered to Wang *rong (the chemicals company) for disposal. Huang *jun, then director of the dyeing company's tank area, knowing that Wang *rong did not have the qualifications for disposal, was responsible for directly coordinating Wang *rong to transport the waste acid, while Wang * was responsible for the payment for the waste acid disposal fees. In September 2013, Wang *rong, knowing that Ding *dong (handled in a separate action) had no qualifications for disposal of waste acid, reached a verbal agreement with Ding *dong on disposal at the cost of CNY 150 per ton, and instructed Xu *mi to drive a tank car to transport waste acid from the dyeing

Tank farm at Nanjing Dyeing Company** (Photo courtesy of the adjudicating court)

company directly to a vessel parked by Ding *dong at the Yiling Wharf in Jiangdu. By May 2014, waste acid delivered to Ding *dong for disposal had totaled 2,828.02 tons. During the period, Ding *dong instructed Sun *shan, Qian *lin and others for multiple times to drive the vessel at night, and discharged 2,698.1 tons of waste acid directly into the riverway of Taidong River and Xintongyang Canal. Between them, Sun *shan was involved in the discharge of 1728.82 tons, and Qian *lin 318.78 tons. Another 129.92 tons of waste acid that Ding *dong had failed to discharge was seized later. The Jiangsu Science and Technology Consulting Center and the Jiangsu Provincial Academy of Environmental Science held upon expert demonstration and analysis that the aforesaid waste acid liquid generated by the dyeing company was hazardous waste mainly composed of sulfuric acid with large quantities of organic matters. The relatively high concentration of the sulfuric acid was strongly corrosive, and extremely harmful to living bodies, water bodies and the environment. The large amount of organic waste remaining in the waste acid would also cause long-term cumulative damage to the biological environment.

[Judgment]

In the trial of first instance, the Primary People's Court of Gaoyou City of Jiangsu Province held that defendant, the dyeing company, knowing that defendant Wang *rong's chemical company had no qualification for disposal of waste acid, delivered waste acid generated during the production process to Wang *rong for disposal, thus violated the environmental law and provisions of the state; defendant Wang *rong, knowing that Ding *dong had no qualification for disposal of waste acid, still transferred the waste acid of the dyeing company to Ding *dong for disposal; defendant Xu *mi, knowing that the items he transported was waste chemical liquid and that Ding *dong might not have the ability to dispose of waste acid, assisted Wang *rong in the transportation; and defendants Sun *shan and Qian *lin, knowing that it was waste chemical liquid, still secretly discharged it against the provisions of the state, and ultimately lead to serious environmental pollution. All of the above constituted the crime of environmental pollution and should be determined as joint crime. While for defendants Wang *and Huang *jun, the directly liable persons in charge of the dyeing company, who should have known that Wang *rong had no qualification for disposal of waste acid, but still arranged transaction within their respective duties, resulting in serious environmental pollution. They should be held criminally liable for the crime environmental pollution. To avoid the high disposal cost of hazardous waste, the dyeing company, knowingly entrusted other entities with no qualifications for disposal to handle the waste, ultimately lead to serious environmental pollution. In consideration of the dyeing company's circumstances of crime and capacity of fine-payment, the court of first instance sentenced the dyeing company to a fine of CNY 20 million and other defendants to imprisonment ranging from one to five years with penalties for the crime of environmental pollution. After the second-instance hearing,

The Yangtze River in Jiangsu province (Photo courtesy of the adjudicating court)

the Yangzhou Intermediate People's Court of Jiangsu Province affirmed the original judgment.

[Significance]

This case is a criminal case of environmental pollution involving water body pollution due to illegal disposal of hazardous waste. The judgment of the case was a successful attempt of the court in appropriately determining the amount of fines to be imposed upon different parties under the principle of suiting punishment to crime. According to the provisions of the Criminal Law of China, the amount of fines shall be determined based on the circumstances of the crime. In terms of fines for an entity, considerations should include the nature of the crime, the amount of illegal gains, the losses caused and other factors. In this case, to avoid the high disposal cost of hazardous waste, the dyeing company, knowing that others had no qualification for disposal, still entrusted disposal, ultimately leading to serious consequence of environmental pollution. The huge amount of disposal expenses avoided should be determined as the gains obtained through the criminal act. Concurrently, the acts also had caused inevitably considerable expenses for the clean-up of the environmental pollution. According to relevant judicial interpretations, public and private property losses should include property losses directly caused by environmental pollution, reduced value because of the environmental pollution, and the expenses needed for necessary measures to prevent pollution expansion and elimination. Therefore, the amount of public and private property losses shall be used as an important parameter in determining the fines. The people's court, taking into full account the capacity of payment of the company, determined the amount of fines based on the illegal gains obtained and the public and private property losses. The Judgment of criminal punishment supported the restoration of the damaged environment, and also served as an effective deterrent to urge other companies to handle hazardous waste in accordance with the law.

[Courts and Members of the Collegial Bench]

Court of First Instance: In Gaoyou Primary People's Court, Jiangsu, before Wu Jiaming, Ji Xiaohong, Chen Zhaohui

Court of Second Instance: In Yangzhou Intermediate People's Court, Jiangsu, before Yin Xiaotao, Li Chunrong, Hao Jiajia

II. Criminal Case with Add-on Civil Public Interest Litigation against He *qiang on Illegal Killing of Endangered Species and Hunting

[Basic Facts]

From November 2014 to January 2015, when collecting fishes in the Dongtinghu National Nature Reserve in Hunan Province, He *qiang and Zhong *jun came to an agreement on killing wild migratory birds by poisoning with fish farmers and their helpers including Fang *hua, Long *ru, Long *ming, Tu *bao, Yu *qiu, Zhang *hai, and Ren *ping. He *qiang provided pesticides for poisoning and was responsible for purchasing and selling of the killed birds. Afterwards, He *qiang and other persons repeatedly killed wild migratory birds in the nature reserve by poisoning, and the killed birds were all purchased by He *qiang and sold to Wang Qianping under the agency of Li *. On January 18, 2015, 63 migratory birds in eight bags successively purchased by He *qiang and Zhong *jun from Fang *hua and Yu *qiu were seized by staff members of the nature reserve administration in the Haoba Wharf located in Junshan District, Yueyang City. It was identified that the aforesaid 63 migratory birds died of poisoning. In particular, 12 cygnets and five white spoonbills were wild animals under state protection (Category II); there were also grey herons, tadorna ferrugineas, eurasian wigeons, anas poecilorhynchas, and night herons, 46 in total, all protected wild animals with important social, economic and scientific research values. It was verified that the total value of the 63 wild migratory birds seized was CNY44,617.

The People's Procuratorate of Yueyanglou District, Hunan Province instituted a public prosecution in the People's Court of Yueyanglou District, Yueyang City on the ground that He *qiang and other six persons committed a crime of illegal hunting and killing of rare and endangered wildlife. The Forestry Bureau of Yueyang City instituted a civil action incidental to criminal proceedings and requested that the seven defendants should jointly compensate for environmental losses of CNY53,553. The People's Procuratorate of Yueyanglou District supported the action instituted by the Forestry Bureau of Yueyang City.

[Judgment]

In the trial of first instance, the Primary

People's Court of Yueyanglou District of Yueyang City, Hunan Province held that: In collusion with Zhong *jun and Fang *hua, He *qiang illegally killed cygnets, white spoonbills, and other wild animals under state protection (Category II) by poisoning in the Dongtinghu National Nature Reserve in Hunan Province; Li * assisted He *qiang in purchasing pesticides and was fully responsible for selling the wild migratory birds killed by poisoning. The acts of He *qiang, Zhong *jun, Fang *hua, and Li * have constituted a crime of illegal killing of rare and endangered wildlife and the circumstances were particularly serious. Incited by He *qiang, Long *ru, Long *ming, and Long Zhen separately hunted and killed wild migratory birds in the national nature reserve, which damaged wildlife resources. With the serious circumstances, their acts constituted a crime of illegal hunting. In the meantime, the criminal acts of He *qiang and Zhong *jun constituted a crime of illegal killing of rare and endangered wildlife and a crime of illegal hunting . They should be convicted and punished according to a heavier crime, namely, the crime of illegal killing of rare and endangered wildlife. In addition, since the criminal acts of He *qiang and other six persons damaged national wildlife resources and made the national property suffer from damage, all parties should assume the compensation liability. The damage was determined as CNY44,617 according to the verified value of the 63 wild migratory birds involved. On the basis of the different roles of the defendants in the crime, He *qiang, Zhong *jun, Fang *hua, and Li * were sentenced to fixed-term

Cygnets (Photo: Zhou Yang)

Milu deer (Père David's Deer) at Dongtinghu National Nature Reserve (Photo: Hunan Daily)

imprisonments ranging from six years to 12 years, in addition to fines for illegal killing of rare and endangered wildlife. Long *ru, Long *, and Long *ming were sentenced to fixed-term imprisonments ranging from one year and two years and two of them were given probation of two years for illegal hunting. He *qiang and other six persons should jointly pay the Forestry Bureau of Yueyang City CNY44,617 as environmental damage compensation. The Yueyang Intermediate People's Court in Hunan Province rejected the appeal filed by some of the defendants and upheld the judgment of the lower court.

[Significance]

This is a civil action incidental to criminal proceedings concerning illegal hunting and killing of rare and endangered wildlife. Imposition of a penalty is an important way of environmental governance. With increasingly stern environmental resource problems, using criminal penalties properly can effectively punish environmental and resource crimes and deter future illegal acts as an important link in protecting the ecosystem and the environment. This case took place in the Dongtinghu National Nature Reserve. While the procuratorial organ instituted a public prosecution, the relevant competent department of environmental resources instituted a civil action incidental to criminal proceedings. The procuratorial organ supported the civil action and both the criminal liability and civil liability of the actors were investigated according to the law. The court of the first instance confirmed the intents of all the seven defendants to kill wild migratory birds in the nature reserve by poisoning, and properly distinguished each defendant's role in convicting them of the crime of killing rare and endangered wildlife and the crime of illegal hunting according to the principle of consistency between subjectivity and objectivity; in addition, the court of first instance distinguished principal offenders from accessory offenders according to the theory of joint crime and separately sentenced the seven defendants to fixed-term imprisonments ranging from one year to 12 years and some of them were given a probation, reflecting several basic principles in environmental and criminal law, including severe punishment for environmental and resource related crimes, the independent status of environmental legal interests, and combining punishment with leniency, giving full play to the deterrent and educational functions of the Criminal Law. In addition, in this case, both the criminal liabilities of defendants for killing wild migratory birds and the civil compensation liability for environmental damages were investigated. It is of good exemplary significance for the co-handling of cases concerning environmental resources-related criminal offense and civil compensation.

[Courts and Members of the Collegial Bench]

Court of First Instance: In Yueyanglou Primary People's Court, Hunan, before Xiao Bingfeng, Li Lin, Wen Jianshe

Court of Second Instance: In Yueyang Intermediate People's Court, Hunan, before Ren Yan, Yu Beibei, et al.

White spoonbills (Photo: Saifuddin Ratlamwala/Pexels)

III. Civil Public Interest Litigation: Jiangsu ** Environmental Protection Federation v. **Chemicals Company for Water Pollution

[Basic Facts]

From January 2012 to February 2013, the defendant, Taixing ** chemical company (hereinafter referred to as "the chemical company") and other five enterprises delivered a total of over 25,000 tons of hazardous waste of hydrochloric acid and waste sulfuric acid generated in the process of production to other companies without the qualification for disposal of hazardous wastes at a price ranging from CNY20 to 100 per ton, and such hazardous wastes were directly discharged into Rutai Canal of Taixing City and Gumagan River of Gaogang District, Taizhou City secretly, causing serious water pollution. An environmental protection federeation based in Taizhou (hereinafter referred to as " the environmental protection federation") requested the court to order that the six defendant enterprises should pay the environmental restoration fee of over CNY160 million and the appraisal and evaluation fee of CNY100,000.

[Judgment]

After the trial of first instance, the Intermediate People's Court of Taizhou City of Jiangsu Province held that: as a legally-established non-profit organization engaging in the cause of environmental protection, the environmental protection federation had the standing to institute an environmental public interest litigation. The six defendant enterprises delivered the by-product acid to companies without qualification and capabilities for disposal of such hazardous waste with a much lower cost than the expense needed for legal disposal of such by-product acid, causing the dumping of a great volume of by-product acid into rivers and serious environmental pollution. Therefore, they should compensate for the damage caused thereby and restore the ecosystem and the environment. The dumping of over 20,000 tons of by-product acid into rivers would inevitably cause serious environmental damage. As the rivers flew, even though the water quality at the location of the dumping took a turn for the better, it did not mean that the environmental status of the rivers have been fully. Under the circumstance where it was difficult to calculate the restoration costs, the ecological and environmental restoration costs should be calculated by adopting the virtual treatment costs method. Therefore, the court rendered a judgment that the six defendant enterprises should pay the environmental restoration costs of over CNY160 million in total and bear the appraisal and evaluation fee of CNY100,000 and the litigation costs. After the trial of the second instance, the High People's Court of Jiangsu Province confirmed the standing of the environmental protection federation. The court also held that there was clear causation between the disposal of the by-product acid by the six defendant enterprises and the environmental damage in the Gumagan River and Rutai Canal. In the judgment of the first instance, the amount of compensation determined was correct and the method for calculating the restoration costs was appropriate. The six defendant enterprises should legally assume the tortious liability for the damage of environmental pollution caused thereby.

Rutai Canal, Jiangsu Province (Photo: The People's Government of Ruyao Municipality)

Court hearing (Photo courtesy of the adjudicating court)

The judgment of the second instance also affirmed that the six defendant enterprises should pay the environmental restoration costs of over CNY160 million but adjusted the methods for performance of obligations - If the six defendant enterprises could make re-use the by-product acids through technical transformation, significantly decrease environmental risks, and received no other environmental punishments within the following year, the technical transformation costs they have paid may be deducted from the environmental restoration costs ordered to be compensated at a share of not more than 40%. Three defendant enterprises have actively performed the entire judgment of second instance. Unsatisfied with the judgment of second instance, the Taixing ** chemical company filed an application for retrial with the Supreme People's Court of the P.R.C.

The Supreme People's Court held that: In cases of environmental pollution, manufacturers of hazardous chemicals and chemical products should perform higher duties of care for their main products and by-products. They should comprehensively understand whether the main products and the by-products generated in the production process were highly hazardous and whether they would cause environmental pollution; They should also be responsible for the manufacturing, sale, transportation, storage, and disposal of their main products to be compliant with the relevant legal provisions, and avoid damage to the environment, including major risks of environmental damage. Although rivers flow and have the capabilities of self-purification, the environmental capacity of one certain river is limited. The dumping of a large volume of by-product acid to water bodies would inevitably cause severe damage to the water quality, aquatic animals and plants in rivers, riverbeds, river banks, and the ecosystem in the downstream rivers. If the restoration failed to be made in a timely manner, the accumulation of pollutants would inevitably exceed the environmental carrying capacity and finally cause irreversible environmental damage. Therefore, the polluters should not be exempted from liability of environmental restoration on the ground that the water quality of part of the water areas had been restored. The Supreme People's Court finally ruled to deny the chemical company's application for retrial.

[Significance]

This case was described as an environmental public interest litigation case of "sky-high" compensation in the media. In this case, a social organization served as plaintiff, the procuratorial organ upheld the action. The case involved a mix of parties, multiple defendants, high amount of compensation determined, as well as explorations and innovations, so is of high reference value. The court of the first instance properly identified the standing of the environmental protection federation as the plaintiff, and determined that the chemical company and other five companies had the subjective intention of illegally disposing of hazardous wastes, objectively caused the consequence of serious environmental pollution, and should assume the liability of compensation for environmental damage and restoration. At the same time, in light of the appraisal conclusion and the expert opinions, the court of the first instance determined the environmental restoration costs, and ordered that the six defendant enterprises should compensate the total environmental restoration costs of over CNY160 million. The court of second instance balanced the needs for survival and development of enterprises and goal of environmental protection, innovated in the payment method of restoration costs, and encouraged enterprises to make more efforts in technical upgrade and assume their subject liability and social liability for environmental protection, properly handled the relations between overall interests and partial interests and between long-term interests and short-term interests. The Supreme People's Court affirmed the court of second instance's innovation in the payment method of restoration costs, encouraged enterprises to actively carry out technical innovations and upgrade, and promoted the improvement of regional ecological and environmental quality. In the meantime, the Supreme People's Court specified that the manufacturers of hazardous chemicals and chemical products should perform higher duties of care in the process of manufacturing and assume more social liability. For river water, an environmental medium with fluidity and self-purification capability, the Supreme People's Court determined the treatment principle of water restoration. In other words, once pollution occurred, the restoration obligations assumed by the polluter should not be affected by the self-improvement of the water environment. This case was of demonstration significance in the handling of water pollution cases.

Taizhou City, Jiangsu Province (Photo: Visual China Group)

[Courts and Members of the Collegial Bench]

Court of First Instance: In Taixing Intermediate People's Court, Jiangsu, before Ji Alin, Ye Zhijun, Cai Peng, Wang Jianxiang, Wang Yaguang

Court of Second Instance: In Jiangsu High People's Court, before Liu Jiangong, Chen Ying, et al.

Retrial: In Supreme People's Court, before Lin Wenxue, Wei Wenchao, Liu Xiaofei, Wu Kaimin, et al.

IV. Series Civil Public Interest Litigation: China ** Environmental Protection Foundation v. Ningxia ** Technology Company for Tengger Desert Pollution

[Basic Facts]

On August 8, 2015, the China **Environmental Foundation (hereinafter referred to as the "the Foundation") filed an action in the Intermediate People's Court of Zhongwei City of Ningxia Hui Autonomous Region and alleged that: in the process of production, Ningxia ** technology company and other seven enterprises directly discharged sewage exceeding the prescribed standards to the evaporation pond in violation of regulations, causing severe pollution of the Tengger Desert. Up to the time of action, the rectification had not been completed yet. The Foundation requested the Court to order that the technology company should (1) stop the illegal environmental pollution activities; (2) eliminate hazards causing the environmental pollution; (3) restore the ecology and environment or establish a special fund for the restoration and entrust a qualified third party to implement the restoration; (4) with respect to claims in items (2) and (3), it was requested that the Court should organize the plaintiff, technical experts, legal experts, NPC members, and CPPCC members to jointly review the elimination and the restoration results; (5) compensate for the ecological function loss until full restoration; and (6) extend a formal apology on national media. The Foundation submitted to the Court its legal registration certificate, which showed that it is a foundation legal person registered with the Ministry of Civil Affairs of the People's Republic of China. The annual review materials from 2010 to 2014 submitted by the Foundation demonstrated that it passed the annual inspections in five consecutive years before filing the public interest litigation. The Foundation also submitted a statement that it had no records of administrative or criminal penalty within the recent five years. Besides, the charter of the Foundation provided that mission is to "widely mobilize the whole society to care and support the cause of biodiversity protection and green development, protect the

Yellow River runs through the Tengger Desert (Photo: robertharding/Alamy Stock Photo)

national strategic resources, promote the building of ecological civilization and harmony between man and nature, and build a better home for humanity." The Foundation also submitted to the Court the relevant evidentiary materials that since its establishment in 1985, it has been engaged in such activities as hosting environmental protection seminars, organizing ecological fieldtrips, launching publicity and education campaigns for environmental protection, and filing civil environmental public interest litigation cases.

[Judgment]

In the trial of first instance, the Intermediate People's Court of Zhongwei City of Ningxia Hui Autonomous Region held that the Foundation could not be deemed as a social organization "specially engaging in the public activities of environmental protection" as prescribed in Article 58 of the Environmental Protection Law. Therefore, it ruled that the foundation had no standing to file the action. The Foundation refused to accept the ruling and appealed. After examination, the High People's Court of Ningxia Hui Autonomous Region ruled to dismiss the appeal and affirmed the original ruling. The Foundation then filed an application for retrial with the Supreme People's Court of the P.R.C.. The Supreme People's Court, in accordance with the law, brought the case to trial and held that: since environmental public interests are inclusive and sharable, it is impossible to determine one specific direct interested party legally. It is therefore necessary to encourage, guide, and regulate social organizations to file environmental public interest litigation in accordance with the law, so as to better bring the functions of environmental public interest litigation into play. In accordance with the provisions of Article 58 of the Environmental Protection Law and Article 4 of the Interpretation of the Supreme People's Court on Several Issues concerning the Application of Law in the Trial of Environmental Civil Public Interests Litigations (hereinafter referred to as the "Interpretation"), the issue of whether the Foundation involved in this case could file an action as a social organization "specially engaged in public activities of environmental protection" should be examined mainly from three aspects, namely, whether its missions and business scope included safeguarding the environmental public interests, whether it actually engaged in public activities of environmental protection, and whether the environmental public interests it safeguarded were related to its missions and business scope. Whether the missions and business scope of a social organization included safeguarding the environmental public interests should be judged according to the content and nature of its work other than just the literal expression. Even though the charter of a social organization did not specifically contain the wording "safeguarding the environmental public interests", if the work content was within the scope of protecting various natural elements impacting the survival and development of mankind and those subject to artificial modification, it should be identified that the missions and business scope of the organization included safeguarding the environmental public interests. The missions in the charter of the Foundation aligned with green development and were closely related to environmental protection, and should be deemed to be within the scope of safeguarding the environmental public interests. Public activities of environmental protection not only include activities directly improving the environment such as tree planting, protection of endangered species, energy conservation and emission reduction, and environmental restoration, but also environmental protection-related publicity and education, research and training, academic exchange, legal aid, public interest litigation, and other activities that were conducive to improving the environmental governance system, enhancing the environmental management capacity, and promoting public consensus on environmental protection in the whole society. Although the relevant evidentiary materials submitted by the Foundation in the trial of first instance, second instance, and retrial was not cross-examined, including the history of the organization, photographs of public activities, and notice on case-filing and acceptance of previous environmental public interest litigation cases, at the stage of case-filing and examination, they were sufficient enough to show that since its establishment in 1985, the Foundation has been actually engaged in environmental protection activities, including hosting environmental protection seminars, organizing ecological fieldtrips, launching publicity and education campaigns on environmental protection, and filing environmental civil public interest litigation, for a long time and was in complaint with the provisions of the Environmental Protection Law and the Interpretation. In the meantime, the aforesaid evidence also proved that the duration in which the Foundation engaged in public activities of environmental protection has been over five years and was in line with the provisions on standings of Article 58 of the Environmental Protection Law that a social organization eligible for civil environmental public interest litigation should engage in public activities of environmental protection for five consecutive years or more. In accordance with the provisions of Article 4 of the Interpretation, the public environmental interests involved in the public interest litigation filed by a social organization should have certain relevance with the missions and business scope of the social organization. Even though the matter instituted by the social organization did not have a direct co-relationship with the missions and business scope of the social organization, if such matter had certain relevance with the environmental elements or the ecological system under the protection of the social organization, the standing of the social organization should be confirmed according to the standard of relevance. This environmental public interest litigation was filed due to pollution of the Tengger Desert. The complex and fragile desert ecological system formed in the interaction between desert biocenosis and the environment required much more cherishment and good care of the mankind during utilization. In the action, the Foundation alleged that the technology company discharged sewage exceeding the prescribed standards to the evaporation pond, which severely damaged the already fragile ecological system of the Tengger Desert. Safeguarding the environmental public interests involved was included in the missions and business scope of the Foundation. In addition, the foundation's legal person registration certificate, the annual review materials, and the statement on no penalty records submitted by the Foundation showed that it matched other requirements for social organizations to file environmental public interest litigation as prescribed in Article 58 of the Environmental Protection Law and Articles 2, 3, and 5 of the Interpretation, and the Foundation had the standing for filing a civil environmental public interest litigation. The Supreme People's Court rendered a retrial ruling to set aside the rulings of the first and second instance and ordered the Intermediate People's Court of Zhongwei City to place the case on file for hearing.

[Significance]

Through the trial of a series of civil public interest litigation over pollution of the Tengger Desert and handling the prominent issues related to the standing of plaintiff in the trial of environmental public interest litigation cases in various regions since the implementation of the newly-revised Environmental Protection Law, the Supreme People's Court determined and described the judicial rules for the application of law regarding the standing of plaintiff as prescribed in Article 58 of the Environmental Protection Law and the Interpretation. It was specified in the retiral ruling that in respect of the standing of a social organization in filing a civil environmental public interest litigation, the social organization should be examined mainly from three aspects, namely, whether its missions and business scope included safeguarding the environmental public interests, whether it actually was engaged in pubic

An oasis in the middle of the Tengger Desert (Photo: Visual China Group)

activities of environmental protection, and whether the environmental public interests it safeguarded in the case involved were related to its missions and business scope. The ruling elaborated that whether the missions and business scope of a social organization included safeguarding the environmental public interests should be judged by the contents of the organization's work other than literal wordings; that public activities of environmental protection not only included activities of directly improving the environment, but also activities conducive to improving the environmental governance system, enhancing the environmental management capabilities, and promoting public consensus on environmental protection; and that even though the matter instituted by the social organization did not have direct co-relation with its missions and business scope, if such matter had certain relevance with the environmental elements or the ecological system under the protection of the social organization, the standing of the social organization should also be affirmed according to the standard of relevance. In this series of cases, the Supreme People's Court specified the standards for standing in civil environmental public interest litigation at the judicial level for the first time, promoted the development of the environmental public interest litigation system. These cases have been published by the Supreme People's Court as guiding cases and served as demonstration for future trials of cases of similar nature.

[Court and Members of the Collegial Bench]

Retrial: In Supreme People's Court, before Liu Xiaofei, Ye Yang, Wu Kaimin

V. Civil Public Interest Litigation: Beijing Chaoyang ** Environmental Research Institute, Fujian ** Environmental Center v. Xie *jin and Three Other Persons for Deforestation

[Basic Facts]

On July 29, 2008, Xie *jin and three others expanded mining outside the area authorized by competent authorities. By stripping away the vegetation of the mountain from top down, dumping the abandoned rocks generated by mining down the mountain, and building a shed under the mine, the defendants seriously destroyed 28.33 mu of woodland vegetation. On July 28, 2014, Xie *jin et al were sentenced to imprisonment for the crime of illegally occupying agricultural land. On January 1, 2015, the Beijing ** Environmental Research Institute and Fujian ** Environmental Center filed a lawsuit, requesting that the four defendants be ordered to restore the forest land vegetation within certain time frame and compensate for the loss of ecological and environmental service functions in the amount of CNY 1.34 million; if the forest land vegetation cannot be restored timely, the defendants shall also pay for the cost of environmental damage restoration of over CNY 1.1 million; they shall also jointly reimburse the plaintiffs for the environmental damage assessment fee, attorney's fee and other reasonable costs incurred in the proceeding.

[Judgment]

Fujian Nanping Intermediate People's Court held in the first instance that Xie *jin and three others occupied forest land for mining, which not only seriously damaged the vegetation of 28.33 mu of forest land, but also caused the loss of ecological services during the period from the damage of forest vegetation to the restoration to the baseline state. Therefore, Xie *jin and other three persons were ordered to restore the function of the damaged 28.33 mu of forest land within five months from the effective date of the judgment, reforest the land and nurture and conserve the

He Zhouping Village, Huaqiao Township, Guangze County, Fujian Province (Photo: Wang Nan)

saplings for three years; if failing to do so, they shall jointly compensate for the environmental damage restoration costs of more than CNY 1.1 million and loss of ecological service function of CNY 1.27 million for in-situ or off-site ecological restoration; they shall also jointly pay the plaintiff the appraisal fee, attorney's fee and other reasonable expenses for the litigation of over CNY 165,000. The Fujian High People's Court upheld the verdict of the first instance.

[Significance]

This case is the first national civil environmental public interest litigation since the revised Environmental Protection Law came into force, It involved the review of the plaintiff's eligibility to sue, the liability for environmental restoration and the compensation for the loss of ecological and environmental service functions. In accordance with Article 58 of the Environmental Protection Law of the People's Republic of China and the Interpretation of the Supreme People's Court on Several Issues Concerning the Application of Law to the Adjudication of Environmental Civil Public Interest Litigation, the court handed down a judgment confirming the standing of the institute and the center to bring the public interest litigation case. The court of the first instance prioritized ecological restoration, ordering the defendants to restore the function of the damaged forest land within a timeframe, reforest the land and nurture and conserve the saplings for three years. The ultimate purpose of restoring the vegetation and the damaged ecosystem is thus fulfilled. The decision has set a precedent by supporting the request for compensation for the loss of service function during the period from when the damage happened till the restoration of land to the baseline state. It raised the cost of ecological damage and highlighted the values of environmental protection.

[Courts and Members of the Collegial Bench]

Court of First Instance: In Nanping Intermediate People's Court, FuJian, before Lin Dongbo, Gan Daixing, Zhang Tinggui, Huang Huiqin, Zhu Feng

Court of Second Instance: In Fujian High People's Court, before Zhu Changlin, Li Heping, Lin Jinbin

He Zhouping Village, Huaqiao Township, Guangze County, Fujian Province (Photo: Wang Nan)

VI. Civil Public Interest Litigation: Jiangsu Xuzhou People's Procuratorate v. Xuzhou ** Paper Company for Water Pollution

[Basic Facts]

The local competent department of environmental protection found multiple times that Xuzhou ** Papermaking Company (hereinafter referred to as "the papermaking Company") discharged production sewage to the Subei Dike River connecting to the Beijing-Hangzhou Canal through privately-set subsurface drainage pipes. The chemical oxygen demand (COD), ammonia nitrogen, total phosphorus, and other pollutant indicators in the sewage exceeded the prescribed standards. Previously, the Environmental Protection Bureau of Tongshan District, Xuzhou City, Jiangsu Province had imposed administrative penalties on the papermaking company twice. On December 28, 2015, as a public interest litigant, the People's Procuratorate of Xuzhou City instituted civil environmental public interest litigation in the Intermediate People's Court of Xuzhou City and requested the Court to order that the papermaking company should restore the environment of the Subei Dike River damaged by the pollution to the original state and compensate for the service function losses during the period from when the damage happened until the full restoration of the river to the original state; if the papermaking company could not restore the environment to the original state, the People's Procuratorate of Xuzhou City requested the Court to order that the company should assume the liability of compensation to pay a cost three to five times of the benchmark restoration cost (benchmark cost: CNY 269,100 per 2600 tons).

[Judgment]

In the trial of first instance, the Intermediate People's Court of Xuzhou City of Jiangsu Province held that: The discharge of sewage by the papermaking company had caused environmental pollution, and the company should assume the liability for environmental pollution. Considering the facts of environmental pollution caused, the intent of the papermaking company, the operation costs of pollution prevention and control facilities, the service functions of the ecological environment,

Sewage discharged through the drain pipe into the river (Photo: Dmitriy Prayzel/Shutterstock)

and the difficulty in ecological restoration, the costs for ecological restoration from the damage happened till full restoration that should be borne by the papermaking company could be calculated based on the ecological function loss during the period. Therefore, the Court rendered a judgment that papermaking company should pay a total of CNY1.0582 million as ecological damage compensation. The papermaking company appealed upon the judgment against the People's Procuratorate of Xuzhou City, public interest litigant in the trial of the first instance. In the trial of the second instance, the High People's Court of Jiangsu Province held that: The fact that the environmental quality of the sewage discharge point has reached the required standard could not serve as the ground for the papermaking company's refusal to bear the cost for ecological restoration. It was not inappropriate for the judgment of the first instance to use 2.035 times as the coefficient in the calculation of the restoration costs based on the method of virtual treatment costs. There were both factual basis and legal basis to use four times of the volume of sewage discharged for the calculation of the environmental restoration costs. The Court rendered a judgment of the second instance to dismiss the appeal and affirm the original judgment.

[Significance]

This case is among the first batch of civil public interest litigation accepted by the people's courts since the Standing Committee of the National People's Congress authorized procuratorial organs to initiate the pilot program of filing public interest litigation and it is also the first case of second instance tried by the people's court where the procuratorial organ initiated the pilot program of instituting public interest litigation. The court of the first instance also attached importance to information disclosure and public participation during the trial. The collegial bench consisted of judges and people's jurors and the court session was live broadcasted to the public in video and texts. During the court hearings, expert witness were invited to raise expert opinions on technical issues, helping the court to make impartial and science-based decisions in environmental cases. In this case, the ecological restoration costs was reasonably determined considering factors including the degree of subjective fault of defendant for its illegal discharge of pollutants, the concealment of its pollutant discharge activities, and the environmental damage consequences. Through the judgment, the costs of law-violation for the polluting enterprise were increased, deterring the illegal discharge of pollutants by the enterprise from the source. In accordance with the Civil Procedure Law and the Decision of the Standing Committee of the National People's Congress on Authorizing the Supreme People's Procuratorate to Launch the Pilot Program of Filing Public Interest Litigations in Some Areas, the court of the second instance tried the case and demonstrated how the rules for such cases function.

[Courts and Members of the Collegial Bench]

Court of First Instance: In Xuzhou Intermediate People's Court, Jiangsu, before Cai Keyong, Li Juan, Chen Hu, Xu Shuqi, Zhou Xiaoyun

Court of Second Instance: In Jiangsu High People's Court, before Chen Ying, Zang Jing, Zhao Li

White Horse Lake of Jiangsu Province (Photo: Huai'an White Horse Lake Tourist Resort Website)

VII. Civil Public Interest Litigation: ** Environment Protection Federation v. Dezhou ** Company for Air Pollution

[Basic Facts]

Domiciled in Dezhou City, Shandong Province, Dezhou ** Co., Ltd. (hereinafter referred to as"** Company") was an enterprise engaging in the manufacturing of glass and highly-processed glass products. Although ** Company invested in the construction of desulfurization and dust removal facilities, there was still constant emission of pollutants exceeding the prescribed standards through two chimneys, causing air pollution and seriously affecting the lives of surrounding residents. It was criticized by the Ministry of Environmental Protection by name and repeatedly penalized by the competent administrative department of environmental protection, but the illegal emission. **Environment Protection Federation (hereinafter referred to as "the Federation") instituted an action in the Intermediate People's Court of Dezhou City and requested the Court to order that ** Company should immediately cease the emission of pollutants to the air exceeding the prescribed standards and add more air pollution prevention

Air pollution
(Photo: Predrag Mladenovic/shutterstock)

Clean air in the downtown area (Photo: Mckyartstudi/Shutterstock)

and control facilities, and should not resume the production and operation until such facilities passed the review and acceptance of the competent environmental authorities and were put into use; ** Company should pay CNY20.4 million (changed to CNY27.46 million during litigation) as compensation for the damage caused by the excessive emission of pollutants and CNY7.8 million for losses caused by its refusal to correct. The aforesaid sums of money should be paid to the special financial account of the local government for air pollution control in Dezhou City; ** Company should extend a formal apology to the public on the media at or above the provincial level; and ** Company should bear the litigation fee, inspection fee, appraisal fee, expert witness fee, lawyers' fee, and other expenses involved in the litigation. After accepting the case, the Intermediate People's Court of Dezhou City of Shandong Province served the complaint for civil action and other materials on claim upon ** Company, made a public announcement on the case filing, and informed the Environmental Protection Bureau of Dezhou City. The People's Government of Dezhou City and the Environmental Protection Bureau of Dezhou City actively supported the trial of this case, and jointly held coordination meetings with the court of the first instance. Through the cooperation and coordination between the judicial organ and the competent administrative department of environmental protection, ** Company closed down all production lines, selected a new site in Tianqu Industrial Park far away from living quarters for residents, and constructed a new plant. In this way, further expansion of pollution and damage was contained and interim measures were taken during the trial of the case when the case was still pending.

[Judgment]

In the trial of first instance, the Intermediate People's Court of Dezhou City of Shandong Province held that during litigation, ** Company drew off the water, suspended production, and ceased the use of the original plant. Hence it may be deemed that ** Company has ceased infringement. Before ceasing the emission of pollutants, ** Company had not been equipped with or had not run desulfuration and denitration facilities, had not been equipped with dust removal facilities or had had dust removal facilities with insufficient processing capacity, and repeatedly emitted such pollutants as sulfur dioxide, nitric oxide, and smoke and dust to the air exceeding the prescribed standards. In particular, sulfur dioxide and nitric oxide were precursors to acid rain. The acid rain formed by the excessive emission of sulfur dioxide and nitric oxide would bring personal injury and property damage to residents and the excessive emission of smoke and dust would affect the atmospheric visibility and air cleanliness. Since ** Company's excessive emission of pollutants resulted in damage to the ecologic added-value of atmospheric environment, it should be liable for ecological and environmental restoration and compensate for losses of service functions during the period from the time when the damage happened to its restoration to the original state. In the meantime, ** Company's excessive emission of pollutants to the atmosphere infringed upon the benefits and interests of the public and it should assume the civil liability for extending a formal apology. Therefore, the Intermediate People's Court of Dezhou City rendered a judgment that ** Company should pay CNY21.9836 million as compensation for losses caused by its excessive emission of pollutants, which would be used for the atmospheric environmental quality restoration; and ** Company should extend a formal apology to the public on the media at or above the provincial level. After the judgment of first instance was pronounced, no party appealed and the judgment has come into force.

[Significance]

The case in Dezhou City is the first public interest litigation case on air pollution in the Beijing-Tianjin-Hebei region and surrounding regions accepted by the people's court since the implementation of the revised Environmental Protection Law. With mobility, the atmosphere itself has certian self-purification functions. The difficulty in the trial of this case was whether an enterprise's excessive emission of pollutants constituted damage to the environment. The judgment of this case specified that the excessive emission of sulfur dioxide, nitric oxide, and dust would affect the ecological service functions of the atmosphere and the emitting enterprise should bear legal liability. The virtual costs of air pollution control may be calculated according to the volume of pollutants emitted by exceeding the prescribed standards and the unit control costs of sulfur dioxide, nitric oxide, and dust and the virtual costs served as basis for compensation for ecological and environmental damage. It was worth approving that during litigation, ** Company voluntarily assumed social responsibility and actively adopted measures to prevent the continuity and expansion of pollution. The conclusion of this case responded to the public concerns over the air pollution control in the Beijing-Tianjin-Hebei region and the surrounding regions in a timely manner and demonstrated a good practice for the control of regional air pollution.

[Court and Members of the Collegial Bench]

Court of First Instance: In Dezhou Intermediate People’s Court, Shandong, before Liu Libing, Zhang Xiaoxue, Gao Xiaomin

VIII. Case of Contractual Disputes: Sichuan ** Mining Company v. Xinjiang * *Resource Investment Company over Mineral Rights

[Basic Facts]

On October 10, 2011, Xinjiang ** Resource Investment Company (hereinafter referred to as "the investment company") signed a "Cooperative Exploration and Development Agreement"(hereinafter referred to as

Tashkurgan County, Xinjiang Uygur Autonomous Region
(Photo: The People's Government of Tashkurgan County)

"the Agreement"with Sichuan ** Mining Company (hereinafter referred to as "the mining company"). It was agreed that the two parties would jointly establish a project company and that the mining company would transfer its exploration rights to the project company when conditions were met at a cost of CNY 35 million compensated by the investment company. Following the agreement, the investment company made the payment of CNY 35 million to the mining company on October 25, 2011. Then on November 22, 2013, the investment company requested to cancel the Agreement on the grounds that the area for cooperative mining exploration was situated in the Tashkurgan Wildlife Nature Reserve in Xinjiang, and the request was declined by the mining company. In order to establish the legality of the Agreement and the invalidity of the request for termination of the contract by the investment company, the mining company filed a lawsuit. The investment company, on the other hand, filed a counterclaim, requesting to cancel the Agreement and that the mining company to return the payment of CNY 35 million and compensate for other losses incurred.

[Judgment]

The High People's Court of Xinjiang Uygur Autonomous Region in its first instance dismissed the investment company's claims, deciding that the request of the investing company to cancel the Agreement was invalid, and that both parties should continue to implement the Agreement. The Supreme People's Court however, in the second instance, held that the mining exploration right of the mining company involved the Tashkurgan Wildlife Nature Reserve, which had been created before the exploration right of the mining company was granted. Both parties were or should have been aware that the

exploration and exploitation of mineral resources were prohibited in nature reserves, according the Cooperative Exploration and Development Agreement. The Agreement was in violation of the restrictive rules of China's Regulation on Nature Reserve. The natural environment, ecology, and the general public's environmental interests and benefits would suffer significantly if the Agreement were determined to be valid and continued to be in effect. Therefore, in accordance with the law, the contract should be void, and the CNY 35 million in cooperative remuneration that the mining company has already received should be returned. As for the compensation for other losses requested by the investment company, part should be covered by the mining company at a reasonable discount, part should be borne by the investment company itself or be resolved after the liquidation of the project company. The decision of the first instance court was overturned.

[Significance]

The conflicts between the needs for environmental conservation and economic development are more frequently seen in special ecosystems such as nature reserves, scenic spots, important ecological functioning areas, eco-environmental sensitive areas, and fragile areas. In hearing and enforcing cases in such areas, the court should adopt different measures, taking into full consideration of the different roles of different functional areas according to the national and provincial land and spatial planning. Priority should be given to the environment's capacity in developing the economy, and in particular, for environmental disputes in areas where development is prohibited or restricted, such as the ecological redline areas, the most stringent protection measures should be put in place. Any mining exploration and exploitation contracts involving the aforementioned areas should be under strict scrutiny of the people's courts, regardless of the approval for the contract from the competent land and resource departments. The contract shall be deemed void if it contravenes with existing laws and harms public interests. The ruling of the case sets a precedent for the trial of validity of contracts involving development and utilization of natural resources.

[Court and Members of the Collegial Bench]

Court of Second Instance: In Supreme People's Court, before Wang Jijun, Yan Jing, Zhu Jing

IX. Case of Damage Compensation: Guizhou ** Eco-farming and Development Company v. Guizhou ** Aluminum Industry Company for Property Damage Compensation

[Basic Facts]

Sturgeon farming is the core business of Guizhou ** Eco-farming and Development Company (hereinafter referred to as"the farming company"). The company uses water from the Gojiazhai Ditch for farming. In October 2014, Guizhou ** Aluminium Company (hereinafter referred to as"the alumimnum company"), constructed a dam to draw water from the Gojiazhai Reservoir's in the upstream. The construction of the dam caused the drop of water quantity of the downstream, affecting the farming company's sturgeon ponds-a considerable number of sturgeon raised by the farming company perished because of severe water shortage and oxygen deprivation between April 21 and 23. The farming company asserted that the aluminum company, in constructing the dam, should have taken adequate remediation measures given its knowledge of the potential impacts to water supply. However in reality, the aluminum company stored water without permission and turned off the water supply for downstream without prior notice, killing sturgeons in large quantity. The farming company filed a lawsuit against the aluminum company before the court, alleging that the aluminum company should be liable for compensation.

Sturgeons
(Photo: DIGITALSHAPE/Shutterstock)

Ecological flow released by the aluminum company to restore water flow downstream
(Photo courtesy of the adjudicating court)

Fish farming (Photo courtesy of the adjudicating court)

[Judgment]

The Qingzhen Primary People's Court of Guizhou Province ruled in the first instance that, the ecological flows of rivers can guarantee the capacity of the rivers for self-purification diffusion, preserve the balance of aquatic ecosystems, and provide the water quality and quantity needed by the aquaculture sector in the reservoir area. Although there is no specific rules for ecological flow in China's law, it is necessary to ensure the minimum discharge flow of hydropower plants in practice. The aluminum company used the water by building the dam without a valid administrative permit for water-taking and proper environmental impact assessment, causing the shortage of ecological flow, leading to decrease in water flow downstream and in the water intake of the sturgeon aqua farm, resulting in suffocation of sturgeons in the pond. The causation between the mortality of the sturgeon raised by the farming company and the water storage of the aluminum company could be established, and the aluminum firm should make up for the farming company's economic loss of CNY 757,158.6. The aluminum company appealed and was dismissed by the Guiyang Intermediate People's Court. The original verdict was maintained.

[Significance]

The Yangtze river basin is abundant with water resources. Thus it is a crucial responsibility of the people's courts to hear matters related to Yangtze river protection and sustainable use in accordance with the law. This case involves the protection and regulation of "ecological flow" in using water resources. It is an infringement dispute resulting from the process of developing and utilizing water resources. Rivers' ecological flow is of significant importance. Water users in upstream areas should protect river ecological flow during the development and use of water resources and should not infringe on the legal rights and interests of downstream beneficiaries of ecological flow in water supply, navigation, irrigation, and breeding. It is necessary to maintain the core functions of aquatic ecosystems throughout the entire basin. In this instance, two companies—a sturgeon farm and an aluminum company—are water users of the Gojiazhai Reservoir and should take, use, and discharge water in line with the legislation.
The aluminum company should be held legally liable for compensation if it damages the legitimate rights and interests of downstream water users by building interception dams illegally in the upper reaches without water taking and using permits the environmental impact assessment. This decision of the court upholds the importance of ecological flow and protects the legitimate rights and interests of ecological flow beneficiaries, providing guidance for the people's courts in hearing disputes involving water use.

[Courts and Members of the Collegial Bench]

Court of First Instance: In Qingzhen Primary People's Court, Guizhou, before Luo Guangqian, Li Yunhe, Zhang Qi

Court of Second Instance: In Guiyang Intermediate People's Court, Guizhou, before Zeng Zhen, Tang Yuping, Ma Jie

X. Case of Hainan ** Water Company v. Hainan ** Environmental Protection Bureau over Administrative Penalty

[Basic Facts]

The Environmental Protection Bureau of Danzhou City held that Hainan ** Water Co., Ltd. (hereinafter referred to as the "** Water Company") was suspected of illegally discharging water pollutant based on a monitoring report issued by the Environmental Monitoring Center of Hainan Province on June 5, 2013 (hereinafter referred to as "No. 153 Monitoring Report"). On April 16, 2014, Danzhou Environmental Protection Bureau issued a warning for administrative penalty to the ** Water Company. Within the statutory time limit, the ** Water Company failed to file an application for a statement of explanation, defending itself, or holding a hearing. As a result, on June 16 of the same year, the Environmental Protection Bureau of Danzhou City issued a Written Decision on Administrative Penalty (No. 47 [2014], Environmental Protection, Danzhou) (hereinafter referred to as the "No. 47 Penalty Decision") requesting ** Water Company should pay a fine of CNY177,719, two times of the regular costs for sewage. Upon reconsideration, the People's Government of Danzhou City affirmed the No. 47 Penalty Decision. The ** Water Company refused to accept the penalty decision and appealed to the Primary People's Court of Danzhou City, requesting the revocation of the No. 47 Penalty Decision.

[Judgment]

In the trial of first instance, the People's Court of Danzhou City of Hainan Province held that: As the competent administrative department of environmental protection in Danzhou City, the Environmental Bureau of Danzhou City had the statutory functions of imposing an administrative penalty on any entity that illegally discharged water pollutants. In accordance with the provisions of Article 34 of the Measures for Environmental Administrative Penalty, sampling was a mandatory procedure of monitoring in this case. However, the Environmental Protection Bureau of Danzhou City failed to provide the sampling record, sampling process, and other relevant evidence and failed to testify the authenticity of the submitted samples, which directly affected the authenticity of the monitoring results. In this case, the Environmental Protection Bureau of Danzhou City failed to

Danzhou City, Hainan Province (Photo: Suxiaojie/Hainan Daily)

collect conclusive evidence for proving the authentic and reliable source of samples, and determined that the ** Water Company discharged excessive sewage only on the basis of the result of the No. 153 Monitoring Report. The main evidence for the decision was insufficient. On June 16, 2014, the Environmental Protection Bureau of Danzhou City imposed another fine on the ** Water Company for its excessive discharge of sewage on January 14 and May 22, 2013. The decision was procedurally illegal. In the No. 47 Penalty Decision, the ** Water Company was only ordered to pay a fine and it was not ordered to make corrections within a prescribed time limit. The administrative penalty was obviously improper. The court of the first instance rendered a judgment that the No. 47 Penalty Decision should be set aside and the Environmental Protection Bureau of Danzhou City should bear the litigation costs. In the trial of the second instance, the Second Intermediate People's Court of Hainan Province held that: The legality of the No. 153 Monitoring Report was the foundation for examining whether the fact-finding in the administrative penalty was clear. Since the sampling procedure in the No. 153 Monitoring Report was illegal, it could not serve as the material evidence for the decision that the ** Water Company committed any environmental violations. Except for the No. 153 Monitoring Report, the Environmental Protection Bureau did not conduct any other investigations and it violated the provisions on separation of investigation and punishment. The procedure was illegal. The material evidence based on which the facts were found in the No. 47 Penalty Decision was insufficient and the application of law was erroneous. The court of the second instance rendered a judgment to dismiss the appeal and affirm the original judgment.

[Significance]

This is a case concerning dispute over an environmental administrative penalty and involves examination and determination for the environmental penalty. It is a model case with guiding significance. In recent years, the administrative law enforcement departments of environmental protection at various levels have exerted more efforts to administrative law enforcement of environmental violations and effectively contained environmental pollution. However, seen from the cases heard by the court relating to environmental administrative penalties, sometimes the procedures for such enforcement decisions are flawed. The problem of "emphasis of results over procedures" exists. In environmental monitoring, the environmental law enforcement department should attach importance to the procedures. In particular, in cases concerning penalties for water pollution, the technical specifications for sampling directly affects the validity of the testing results. Therefore, the Measures for Environmental Administrative Penalty specifically provided procedures for investigation and sampling on site – it is necessary to keep the sampling records or the sampling process should be included in inspection reports. The sampling may be recorded by photographs, recording, and other means. Since the Environmental Protection Bureau of Danzhou City failed to provide the sampling record, the sampling process, and other relevant evidence and failed to prove the legality of its sampling procedure, the people's court determined that the No. 153 Monitoring Report could not serve as the material evidence for the fact that the ** Water Company had environmental violations and the No. 47 Penalty Decision should be revoked according to the law. The judgment of this case demonstrated supervision of the people's court over environmental administrative law enforcement and it plays a positive role in promoting the competent environmental administrative authorities in exercising the administrative penalty in a standardized manner, contributing to law-based administration.

[Courts and Members of the Collegial Bench]

Court of First Instance: In Danzhou Primary People's Court, Hainan, before Wang Qinghua, Wang Bo, Liu Yaoxiong

Court of Second Instance: In Hainan Second Intermediate People's Court, Hainan, before Zhang Dexiong, Wen Kuixing, Liu Xia

中国具有影响力环境资源案件

（第一辑）

Influential Environment and Resources Cases in China

(Volume I)

封面：长江

摄影：Leon Huang/Pexels

Cover: Yangtze River

Photo: Leon Huang/Pexels

图书在版编目（C I P）数据

中国具有影响力环境资源案件. 第一辑 : 汉文、英文 / 中华人民共和国最高人民法院环境资源审判庭编著. -- 北京 : 人民法院出版社, 2023.5
ISBN 978-7-5109-3043-0

Ⅰ. ①中… Ⅱ. ①中… Ⅲ. ①环境保护法－审判－案例－中国－汉、英 Ⅳ. ①D922.680.5

中国国家版本馆CIP数据核字(2023)第016071号

中国具有影响力环境资源案件（第一辑）
中华人民共和国最高人民法院环境资源审判庭　编著

责任编辑　张　艺
执行编辑　沈洁雯
装帧设计　尹苗苗　鲁　静
出版发行　人民法院出版社
地　　址　北京市东城区东交民巷 27 号（100745）
电　　话　（010）67550667（责任编辑）　67550558（发行部查询）
　　　　　65223677（读者服务部）
客服 QQ　2092078039
网　　址　http://www.courtbook.com.cn
E-mail　courtpress@sohu.com
印　　刷　北京瑞和祥云印刷技术服务有限公司
经　　销　新华书店

开　　本　787 毫米 ×1092 毫米　1/16
字　　数　108 千字
印　　张　5.5
版　　次　2023 年 5 月第 1 版　2023 年 5 月第 1 次印刷
书　　号　ISBN 978-7-5109-3043-0
定　　价　68.00 元